Signing Around Town

SIGN LANGUAGE FOR KIDS

by Kathryn Clay

illustrated by Michael Reid

Consultant: Kari Sween
Adjunct Instructor of
American Sign Language
Minnesota State University, Mankato

CAPSTONE PRESS
a capstone imprint

TABLE OF CONTENTS

How to Use This Guide

This book is full of useful words in both English and American Sign Language (ASL). The English word and sign for each word appear next to the picture. Arrows are used to show movement for some signs.

Most ASL signs are understood wherever you go. But some signs may change depending on where you are. It's like having a different accent.

For example, New Yorkers sign "pizza" like this:

People in other places might sign "pizza" like this:

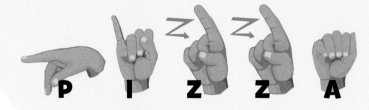

or this:

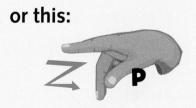

People will not understand you if they can't see your signs. Make sure your hands are always in view when signing with someone. Don't be afraid to ask people to slow down or sign again if you don't understand a sign.

Brief Introduction to American Sign Language (ASL)

Many people who are deaf or hard of hearing use ASL to talk. Hearing people may also learn ASL to communicate with deaf friends and family members.

Signs can be very different from one another. Signs may use one or both hands. Sometimes signs have more than one step. For other signs, you must move your entire body. If there is no sign for a word, you can fingerspell it.

People use facial expressions when they sign. They smile when signing good news. They frown when signing sad news. Body language is also important. Someone might sign slowly to show that he or she is very tired.

It's important to remember that learning to sign is like learning any language. ASL becomes easier with practice and patience.

Alphabet Chart

ASL has a sign for every letter of the English alphabet. If there is no sign for a word, you can use letter signs to spell out the word. Fingerspelling is often used to sign the names of people and places.

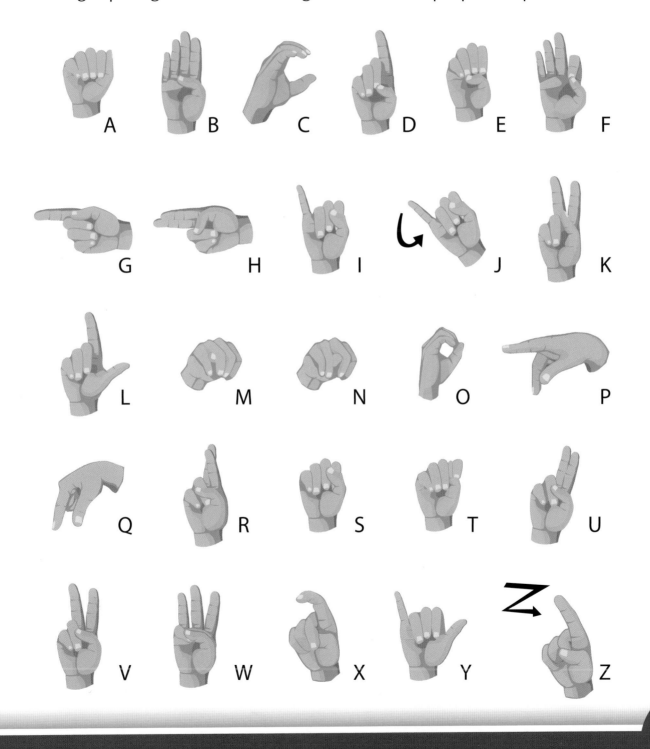

TRANSPORTATION

Move fist forward and back.

car — Move hands as if driving a car.

bus — Fingerspell B-U-S.

truck — Fingerspell T-R-U-C-K.

bicycle Move hands in circles like the pedals of a bike.

train Slide fingers back and forth.

boat Cup hands and move forward.

airplane Point thumb, index, and pinky fingers. Move hand forward.

street Move hands forward.

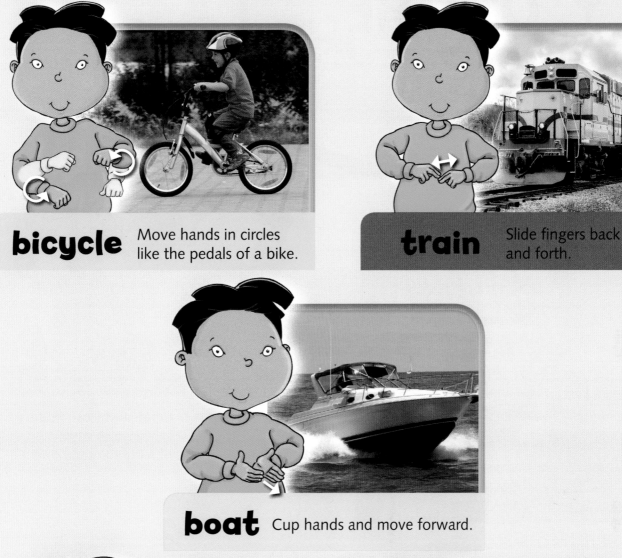

ON THE FARM

Slide thumb across chin.

tractor — Make T shapes and move hands as if driving a tractor.

sheep — Open and close fingers like scissors while moving hand up arm.

farmer
1. Slide thumb across chin.
2. Open hands and move them down body.

pig Put hand on chin and move fingers up and down.

horse Bend first two fingers.

barn Fingerspell B-A-R-N.

chicken Open and close fingers.

cow Make Y shape and wiggle pinky.

AT A RESTAURANT

Make R shape and touch both sides of chin.

menu
1. Move hand down palm twice.
2. Open hands like opening a book.

server
1. Move hands forward.
2. Open hands and move them down body.

salt Wiggle fingers.

pepper Make F shape and shake hand twice.

eat Bring fingers to mouth.

chef
1. Move hand back and forth.
2. Open hands and move them down body.

AT THE DOCTOR'S OFFICE

1. Make D shape and bring hand to wrist.
2. Make O shapes and cross hands.

nurse   Place two fingers on wrist.

sick   Wiggle middle fingers on forehead and stomach.

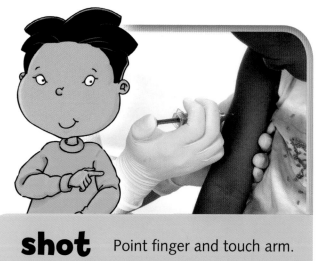

shot   Point finger and touch arm.

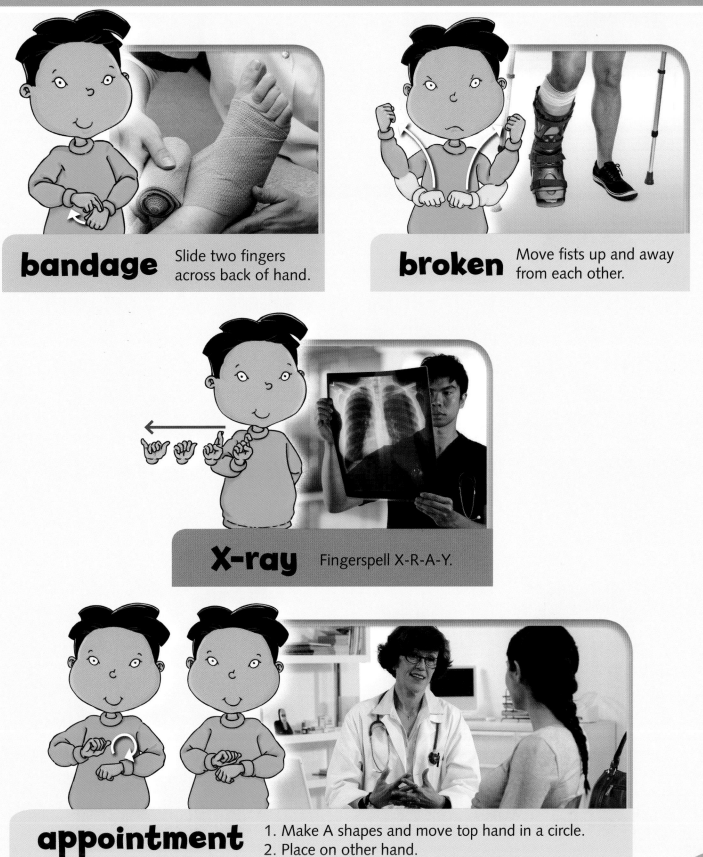

bandage Slide two fingers across back of hand.

broken Move fists up and away from each other.

X-ray Fingerspell X-R-A-Y.

appointment
1. Make A shapes and move top hand in a circle.
2. Place on other hand.

AT THE ZOO

Fingerspell Z-O-O.

elephant Move hand down and away from nose.

lion Curve hand and slide over head.

giraffe Make G shape and move up neck.

penguin Place hands at hips and waddle.

alligator Open and close curved hands.

shark Place hand on top of head like a fin.

monkey Scratch sides twice.

bear Cross hands and scratch chest twice.

zebra Bend fingers and make stripes on chest.

AT THE STORE

Make flat O shapes and move fingers up.

shopping/buy Move top hand away from palm.

money Bring hand to palm.

dollar Slide fingers along top of other hand and into a fist.

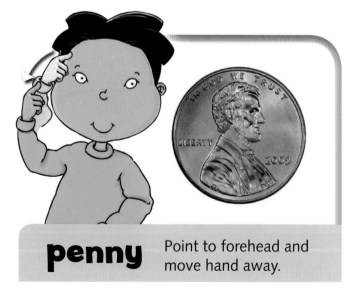

penny Point to forehead and move hand away.

quarter   1. Point to forehead. 2. Wiggle middle finger.

dime   1. Point to forehead. 2. Make a fist and wiggle thumb.

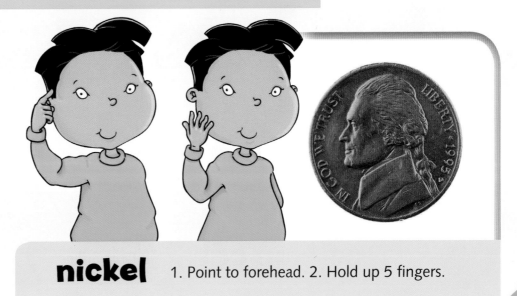

nickel   1. Point to forehead. 2. Hold up 5 fingers.

AT THE CARNIVAL

Bend fingers and move in small circles.

ticket Bend fingers and slide into pinky.

scream Curl hands and move away from mouth.

cotton candy Twist finger at corner of mouth.

roller coaster

Move hand up and down.

haunted house

1. Shake hands.
2. Touch fingertips and move hands down.

popcorn

1. Make fists.
2. Point one finger at a time, back and forth.

AT THE BEACH

Move hands up and down like waves.

towel Move fists back and forth.

water Make W shape and tap mouth twice.

sand Rub fingers together.

whistle Bring two fingers to mouth.

sunglasses

1. Open fist.
2. Close fingers at side of face.

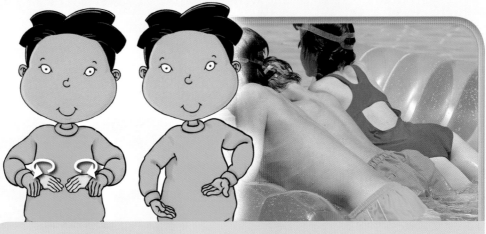

swimsuit

1. Move hands in small circles.
2. Slide hands along chest and waist.

lifeguard

1. Make L shapes and move up chest.
2. Cross hands and make G shapes.

MORE PLACES TO VISIT

bank Fingerspell B-A-N-K.

park Fingerspell P-A-R-K.

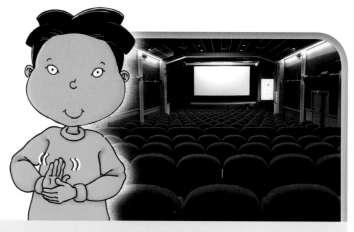

movie theater Move hand back and forth.

hospital Draw a cross on shoulder.

mall Fingerspell M-A-L-L.

grocery store

1. Bring fingers to mouth.
2. Move fingers forward twice.

hair salon

1. Make cutting sign. 2. Open hands and move them down body.

gas station

1. Bring thumb into fist.
2. Move fingers forward twice.

COMMUNITY HELPERS

Place fist on palm and move hands up.

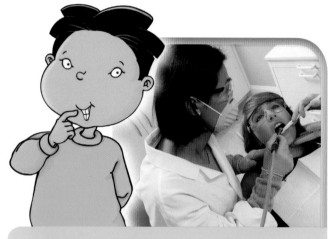

dentist Bring finger to mouth.

firefighter Tap forehead twice.

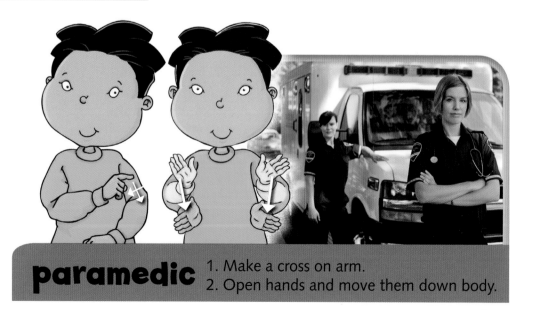

paramedic 1. Make a cross on arm.
2. Open hands and move them down body.

police officer
Make C shape and tap chest twice.

veterinarian
Fingerspell V-E-T.

mail carrier
1. Bring thumb to palm.
2. Open hands and move them down body.

SPORTS

Move thumbs back and forth.

football Lace fingers together twice.

baseball Move hands like swinging a bat.

hockey Curl finger and slide along palm.

26

basketball Move wrists forward twice.

soccer Hit bottom hand twice.

gymnastics Move fingers in a circle around index finger.

tennis Move wrist back and forth like swinging a tennis racquet.

swimming Move hands in small circles.

EXERCISE

Move fists back and forth.

ice skate

Bend fingers and move hands back and forth.

roller skate

Bend two fingers and move hands back and forth.

run Hook thumb and index finger and move hands forward.

jump Bounce two fingers up and down on palm.

walk Move hands up and down like feet walking.

dance Move fingers back and forth on palm.

29

GLOSSARY

accent—the way people say words differently based on where they live

body language—the act of sharing information by using gestures, movements, and facial expressions

communicate—to share thoughts, feelings, or information

deaf—unable to hear

facial expression—feelings shared by making different faces; making an angry face to show you are mad, for example

BOOKS IN THIS SERIES

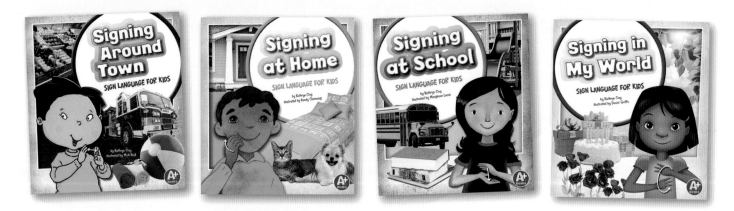

READ MORE

Nelson, Michiyo. *Sign Language: My First 100 Words.*
New York: Scholastic, 2008.

Petelinsek, Kathleen, and E. Russell Primm. *Home=Casa.*
Talking Hands. Chanhassen, Minn.: The Child's World, 2005.

Schaefer, Lola M. *Some Kids Are Deaf.*
Mankato, Minn.: Capstone Press, 2008.

INTERNET SITES

FactHound offers a safe, fun way to find Internet sites related to this book. All of the sites on FactHound have been researched by our staff.

Here's all you do:

Visit *www.facthound.com*

Type in this code: 9781620650530

A+ Books are published by Capstone Press,
1710 Roe Crest Drive, North Mankato, Minnesota 56003
www.capstonepub.com

Library of Congress Cataloging-in-Publication Data
Signing around town : sign language for kids / by Kathryn Clay.
   pages cm.—(A+ books. Time to sign)
Summary: "Illustrations of American Sign Language, along with labeled photos,
introduce children to words and phrases useful for signing around town."
—Provided by publisher.
ISBN 978-1-62065-053-0 (library binding)
ISBN 978-1-4765-3358-2 (ebook PDF)
1. American Sign Language—Juvenile literature. 2. English language—Alphabet—Juvenile literature. I. Title.
   HV2480.C53 2014
   372.6—dc23   2013010647

Editorial Credits
Tracy Davies McCabe, designer; Svetlana Zhurkin, media researcher;
Kathy McColley, production specialist

Photo Credits
Dreamstime: Americanspirit, 25 (bottom), Crazy80frog, 28 (bottom), Dimistudio, 18 (bottom), Greenland, 7 (top left), Ivan Sgualdini, 20 (top left); iStockphotos: Bastun, 3, 5, Christopher Futcher, 27 (top left), John Roman, 25 (top), kali9, 11 (bottom), Kathleen Van Hoffen, 26 (bottom right), Tony Tremblay, 23 (bottom), YinYang, 22 (top); Shutterstock: Africa Studio, 11 (top), Agnieszka Guzowska, 14 (top left), Albert Pego, 7 (top right), Andresr, 27 (bottom left), Angelo Gilardelli, 23 (top), auremar, 8 (bottom), 13 (bottom), bikeriderlondon, 24 (bottom right), Christopher Parypa, 7 (bottom left), Cloudia Newland, 22 (middle left), Creatista, 29 (bottom right), dotshock, 25 (middle), dw1, 7 (bottom right), dyoma, 9 (top left), E. Sweet, 15 (top left), EcoPrint, 14 (bottom right), Fedor Kondratenko, cover (top left), FikMik, 19 (middle), Gemenacom, 23 (middle), Gerard Koudenburg, 28 (top), Goce Risteski , 20 (top right), Golden Pixels, 10 (bottom), Habrda, 22 (middle right), IDAL, 8 (top right), Igor Terekhov, 20 (bottom right), ingridat, 13 (top right), Ivonne Wierink, cover (bottom right), Jaimie Duplass, 12 (bottom left), javarman, 6 (bottom right), Johnny Habell, 6 (left), Juriah Mosin, 18 (top right), Karramba Production, 10 (top), Kellis (whistle), cover, LeonP, 14 (top right), Lucky Business, 8 (top left), Lucy Clark, 14 (bottom left), magicoven, 17 (top and middle), MaszaS, 21 (middle), Miriam Doerr, 13 (top left), Monkey Business Images, 12 (top left), 16 (top left), 24 (top right), 29 (top left and bottom left), Odua Images, 29 (top right), PaulPaladin, 16 (bottom left), Pavel L Photo and Video, 22 (bottom right), Pavel Vakhrushev, 20 (bottom left), Pete Spiro, 16 (bottom right), Peter Clark, 21 (top), Racheal Grazias, 19 (top), Ralf Hirsch, 15 (top right), Ramona Heim, 9 (bottom left), Rob Marmion, 27 (top right), Rob Wilson, cover (middle right), Robyn Mackenzie, 16 (top right), Scott Prokop, 9 (middle), Sergey Peterman, 6 (top right), Shi Yali, 19 (bottom), smereka, 9 (top right and bottom right), soloir, 27 (middle), Sonya Etchison, 26 (left), Stephen Mahar, 22 (bottom left), Stuart Jenner, 13 (middle), Studio DMM Photography, Designs & Art, 18 (top left), Susan Leggett, 26 (top right), Suzanne Tucker, 27 (bottom right), Thomas M. Perkins, 12 (right), tratong, 11 (middle), 15 (bottom right), Tyler Olson, 24 (left), Ugur Anahtarci, 7 (middle), Valery Shanin, 15 (bottom left), Vladimir Wrangel, 17 (bottom), york777, 21 (bottom); Svetlana Zhurkin, 15 (middle)

Note to Parents, Teachers, and Librarians
This accessible, visual guide uses full color photographs and illustrations and
inviting content to introduce young readers to American Sign Language.
The book provides an early introduction to reference materials and encourages
further learning by including the following sections: Table of Contents, Alphabet
Chart, Glossary, Read More, and Internet Sites.

Printed in the United States of America in North Mankato, Minnesota.
032013   007223CGF13